Taxes Made Simple:

Income Taxes
Explained in 100 Pages or Less

Disclaimer

This book is not intended to be a substitute for personalized advice from a professional accountant or attorney. Nothing contained within this text should be construed as tax advice. The publisher and author make no representation or warranty as to this book's adequacy or appropriateness for any purpose. Similarly, no representation or warranty is made as to the accuracy of the material in this book.

Purchasing this book does not create any client relationship or other advisory, fiduciary, or professional services relationship with the publisher or with the author. *You alone* bear the *sole* responsibility of assessing the merits and risks associated with any financial decisions you make. And it should always be kept in mind that any investment can result in partial or complete loss.

Taxes Made Simple:

Income Taxes
Explained in 100 Pages or Less

Mike Piper, CPA

Why is there a light bulb on the cover?

In cartoons and comics, a light bulb is often used to signify a moment of clarity or sudden under-standing—an "aha!" moment. My hope is that the books in the *...in 100 pages or less* series can help readers achieve clarity and understanding of topics that are often considered complex and confusing—hence the light bulb.

Dedication

For the lifelong student.

Your Feedback is Appreciated!

As the author of this book, I'm very interested to hear your thoughts. If you find the book helpful, please let me know. Alternatively, if you have any suggestions of ways to make the book better, I'm eager to hear that, too.

Finally, if you're unhappy with your purchase for any reason, let me know, and I'll be happy to provide you with a refund of the current list price of the book (limited to one refund per title per household).

You can reach me at: mike@simplesubjects.com.

Best Regards,
Mike Piper, CPA

Table of Contents

Part One
Basic Concepts

Part Two
Taxable Income and Taxable Gains

Part Three
Important Deductions and Credits

Part Four
Other Important Things to Know

Introduction

Like the other books in the *...in 100 Pages or Less* series, this book is based on the assumptions that:

a) You're looking to gain a basic understanding of the book's topic (in this case, income taxes), and
b) You don't relish the thought of spending a great deal of time on the effort.

If that's not the case, and you *are* looking for something that's going to turn you into an expert on the topic of income taxes, then you've got the wrong book. Save yourself some time, and look for a different book instead.

Why Bother Learning This Stuff?

The fact that you're holding this book suggests that you appreciate the value of (at least) a basic understanding of taxation. Still, I want to touch briefly upon one point that many people overlook.

What many people misunderstand about taxation is the fact that (even if they don't prepare their own tax returns every year) a little bit of tax knowledge can be quite valuable. The reason is that, by the time your accountant is preparing your tax return, it's frequently too late to do any of the things that you could have done over the course of the year to reduce your tax burden.

The Goal

Ideally, by the time you're finished reading:

- You'll be familiar with income tax terminology,
- You'll understand how all the variables interact to determine how much you get back or owe each tax season,
- You'll be aware of a few strategies to help reduce your taxes, and
- Depending upon your interest level and the complexity of your return, you might find that you're capable of preparing your own tax return next season.

How We're Going to Get You There

This book is broken down into four parts:

1. A quick run-through of the basics (such as the difference between deductions and credits),

2. A look at the different types of taxable income and gains, and how each is taxed,
3. An explanation of several important deductions and credits that could help you reduce your taxes, and
4. An overview of a handful of other topics such as state taxes and the alternative minimum tax.

So without further ado...

PART ONE

The Basics

CHAPTER ONE

Income Tax:
It's Progressive!

The federal income tax is referred to as a "progressive tax." Of course, it's not progressive in the same way that a social movement could be said to be progressive. What the term means in this case is that, as your taxable income increases, so does the rate at which you are taxed.

People will often make statements such as, "I'm in the 22% tax bracket." For example, as you can see on the next page, a single person with a taxable income of $40,000 would be in the 22% tax bracket.[1] People frequently misunderstand this to mean that all of the person's income is taxed at a rate of 22%. In reality, the person's overall federal income tax rate will be much lower.

---

[1] Tax brackets, like many other parts of the tax code, change on a yearly basis to adjust for inflation.

Single (2018)

Taxable income[1]:	The tax is:
$0 - $9,525	10% of the amount over $0
$9,526 - $38,700	$952.50 plus 12% of the amount over $9,525
$38,701 - $82,500	$4,453.50 plus 22% of the amount over $38,700
$82,501 - $157,500	$14,089.50 plus 24% of the amount over $82,500
$157,501 - $200,000	$32,089.50 plus 32% of the amount over $157,500
$200,001 - $500,000	$45,689.50 plus 35% of the amount over $200,000
$500,001+	$150,689.50 plus 37% of the amount over $500,000

EXAMPLE: Samantha's 2018 taxable income is $40,000. This puts her in the 22% tax bracket. If that meant that all of her income was taxed at 22%, she would be paying $8,800 in federal income taxes. Instead, she'll be paying much less. Samantha will actually end up paying $4,739.50, calculated as follows:

1) Her first $9,525 of taxable income is taxed at 10%. ($952.50 of tax)

---

[1] "Taxable income" refers to the amount that's left after subtracting your deductions from your total income.

2) From $9,526 to $38,700 she's taxed at 12%. ($3,501 of tax)
3) From $38,701 to $40,000 Sam is taxed at 22%. ($286 of tax)
4) $952.50 + $3,501 + $286 = $4,739.50.

Filing Status

Your tax bracket depends upon two things: your taxable income and your filing status. The options for filing status are:

1. Single,
2. Married Filing Jointly,
3. Married Filing Separately,
4. Head of Household, and
5. Qualifying Widow(er) with Dependent Child.

Your filing status is based upon your marital and family situation on the *last* day of the tax year. If on the last day of the tax year, multiple filing statuses apply to you, you are allowed to choose between them.

Single
(see previous tax bracket table)
For unmarried taxpayers.

Married Filing Jointly

For married couples who file a joint return that includes all of their combined income, deductions, and credits.

Married Filing Jointly (2018)

Taxable income:	The tax is:
$0 - $19,050	10% of the amount over $0
$19,051 - $77,400	$1,905 plus 12% of the amount over $19,050
$77,401 - $165,000	$8,907 plus 22% of the amount over $77,400
$165,001 - $315,000	$28,179 plus 24% of the amount over $165,000
$315,001 - $400,000	$64,179 plus 32% of the amount over $315,000
$400,001 - $600,000	$91,379 plus 35% of the amount over $400,000
$600,001+	$161,379 plus 37% of the amount over $600,000

Married Filing Separately

For married couples who file separate returns. For the most part, this isn't a beneficial thing to do. Often, married couples who file separate returns are doing so because they are, in fact, separated (though still married), not because of any tax benefit to be gained.

Married Filing Separately (2018)

Taxable income:	The tax is:
$0 - $9,525	10% of the amount over $0
$9,526 - $38,700	$952.50 plus 12% of the amount over $9,525
$38,701 - $82,500	$4,453.50 plus 22% of the amount over $38,700
$82,501 - $157,500	$14,089.50 plus 24% of the amount over $82,500
$157,501 - $200,000	$32,089.50 plus 32% of the amount over $157,500
$200,001 - $300,000	$45,689.50 plus 35% of the amount over $200,000
$300,001+	$80,689.50 plus 37% of the amount over $300,000

Head of Household

Unmarried taxpayers who support one or more dependents may be able to file as head of household. In order to qualify you must:

- Be unmarried on the last day of the year,
- Pay more than half of the cost of keeping up a home for the year, and
- Have had a "qualifying dependent" live with you for more than half of the year. [1]

Head of Household (2018)

Taxable income:	The tax is:
$0 - $13,600	10% of the amount over $0
$13,601 - $51,800	$1,360 plus 12% of the amount over $13,600
$51,801 - $82,500	$5,944 plus 22% of the amount over $51,800
$82,501 - $157,500	$12,698 plus 24% of the amount over $82,500
$157,501 - $200,000	$30,698 plus 32% of the amount over $157,500
$200,001 - $500,000	$44,298 plus 35% of the amount over $200,000
$500,001+	$149,298 plus 37% of the amount over $500,000

---

[1] For more information about qualifying dependents, see Publication 501: irs.gov/publications/p501/

Qualifying Widow(er) with Dependent Child

In the year of your spouse's death, you can file as married filing jointly. For the two following years, you can file as a qualifying widow(er) with dependent child if you meet the following requirements:

- You were eligible to file a joint return with your spouse in the year of his/her death,
- You have not remarried,
- You have a dependent child or stepchild,
- The child lived in your home all year, and
- You paid more than half of the cost of keeping up the home over the course of the year.

Filing as a qualifying widow(er) with dependent child allows you to use the married filing jointly tax brackets and the married filing jointly standard deduction (explained in Chapter 2).

What's a Marginal Tax Rate?

When reading about taxes, you'll often come across the term "marginal tax rate." The term refers to the tax rate that you would pay on one additional dollar of income. In most cases, your marginal tax rate is simply the highest tax bracket that your taxable income reaches.

EXAMPLE: Lauren is single, and her taxable income is $60,000. Therefore, her marginal tax rate is 22%.

Her employer offers her a $10,000 raise in exchange for accepting some additional responsibilities at work. Because Lauren's marginal tax rate is 22%, she knows she'll only get to keep 78% of the extra income. The after-tax value of the proposed raise is only $7,800.[1]

What's an Effective Tax Rate?

Your "effective tax rate" is different from your marginal tax rate. Your effective tax rate is the total amount of income tax you pay, divided by your taxable income. To use our example of Samantha from earlier in the chapter, her effective tax rate would be 11.85%, calculated as $4,739.50 (her total income tax, as calculated using the table

---

[1] In reality, it will be even lower, because she will also have to pay payroll taxes and, most likely, state incomes taxes on the additional income.

earlier in the chapter), divided by $40,000 (her taxable income).[1]

Effective tax rates (unlike marginal tax rates) aren't terribly important from a personal financial planning perspective. Rather, they're typically discussed in a broad economic/political context—with certain groups arguing, for example, that high-income taxpayers should have a higher (or lower) effective tax rate.

---

[1] Sometimes, effective tax rates are calculated to include state income taxes and/or payroll taxes in addition to federal income taxes. They can also be calculated using total income (that is, income before subtracting deductions, which we'll discuss in the next chapter) as the denominator rather than taxable income.

Chapter 1 Simple Summary

- The federal income tax is a progressive tax, meaning that the more you earn, the higher your tax rate.

- The amount of tax you must pay depends not just on your taxable income, but also on your filing status (single, married filing jointly, etc.).

- Your marginal tax rate is the rate of tax you would pay on one additional dollar of income.

- Your effective tax rate is your total income tax, divided by your taxable income.

- Due to the progressive structure of our income tax, a person's effective tax rate will be lower than would seem to be indicated by the statement, "I'm in the ___% tax bracket."

CHAPTER TWO

Deductions and Credits: What's the Difference?

In short, the difference between deductions and credits is that deductions reduce your taxable *income*, while credits reduce your *tax*.

Deductions

Deductions generally arise from your expenses. For example, a deduction is allowed for interest paid on student loans.

EXAMPLE: Carlos is in the 12% tax bracket. Over the course of the year, he paid $2,000 in student loan interest. This $2,000 decrease in his taxable income will save him $240 in taxes ($2,000 x 12%).

Types of Deductions

Deductions are often grouped into two categories:

1. "Above the line" deductions, and
2. "Below the line" deductions (also referred to as "itemized" deductions).

Every year, you can claim all of the above the line deductions for which you qualify, as well as:

1. The itemized deductions for which you qualify, *or*
2. A fixed amount known as the "standard deduction." (In 2018, the standard deduction is $12,000 for a single taxpayer or $24,000 for a married couple filing jointly.)

Here's how it looks mathematically:

Total income (sum of all of your income)
– <u>Above the line deductions</u>
= Adjusted gross income ← "The Line"
– <u>Standard deduction *or* itemized deductions</u>
= Taxable income

A key point here is that above the line deductions are always valuable, whereas itemized deductions are only valuable if and to the extent that they (in total) exceed your standard deduction amount.

That is, if your itemized deductions in a given year are less than the standard deduction, you'll simply claim the standard deduction in that year rather than using your itemized deductions. And your itemized deductions will therefore not provide you with any tax savings.

Some common above the line deductions include contributions to a traditional IRA, contributions to a health savings account (HSA), and interest paid on student loans. We'll be discussing each of these deductions in more depth later.

Common itemized deductions include charitable contributions, the interest on a home mortgage, and medical/dental expenses.[1]

EXAMPLE: Eddie is a single taxpayer. During the year he contributes $3,000 to a traditional IRA, and he makes a charitable contribution of $1,000 to the Red Cross. He has no other deductions, and his income (before deductions) is $50,000.

The IRA contribution is an above the line deduction, and the charitable donation is an itemized deduction.

Using our equation from above, we get this:

---

[1] We will discuss specific itemized deductions in later chapters. Also, you can see the instructions to Schedule A for more information:
irs.gov/pub/irs-pdf/i1040sca.pdf

Total income	$50,000
– Above the line deductions	– $3,000
= Adjusted gross income	= $47,000
– Standard deduction	– $12,000
= Taxable Income	= $35,000

Important observations:

1. Eddie's itemized deductions ($1,000) are less in total than his standard deduction ($12,000). As such, Eddie's charitable contribution doesn't provide him with any tax benefit, because he'll use his standard deduction instead of his itemized deductions.
2. Eddie's above the line deduction provides a tax benefit even though he's using the standard deduction.

Again, itemized/below the line deductions only help when they add up to an amount greater than your standard deduction. Above the line deductions, on the other hand, are always beneficial.

Credits

Unlike deductions, credits reduce your taxes directly, dollar for dollar. After determining the total amount of tax you owe, you then subtract the dollar value of the credits for which you are eligible. This makes credits particularly valuable.

Credits arise from a number of things. Most often, they are the result of the taxpayer doing something that Congress has decided is beneficial for the community. For example, you are allowed a credit of up to $2,500 for paying "qualified education expenses" for yourself, your spouse, or one of your dependents. If you meet the requirements to claim the maximum credit, your *tax* (not taxable income) will be reduced by $2,500.[1]

"Pre-Tax Money"

You'll often hear the term "pre-tax money," generally used in a context along the lines of, "You can pay for [something] with pre-tax money." This means one of two things:

1. The item is deductible, or
2. The item can be paid for automatically in the form of a payroll deduction.

The reason these situations are sometimes referred to as "pre-tax" is that you get to spend this money before the government takes its cut. This makes it more cost-effective for you.

---

[1] This credit is discussed in more detail in Chapter 9.

You may, from time to time, run across people who are under the impression that something is free simply because it's deductible or because they were allowed to spend pre-tax money on it. This is a severe misunderstanding. Being able to spend pre-tax money on something is more akin to getting a discount on the item than it is to getting the item for free.

Chapter 2 Simple Summary

- Deductions reduce your taxable income. Aside from the standard deduction, deductions generally arise from your expenses.

- Each year, you can use *either* your standard deduction *or* the sum of all your itemized (below the line) deductions.

- Above the line deductions are particularly valuable because you can use them regardless of whether you use your standard deduction or itemized deductions.

- Credits, unlike deductions, reduce your tax directly (as opposed to reducing your taxable income). Therefore, a credit is more valuable than a deduction of the same amount.

CHAPTER THREE

Calculating Your Refund
(or Lack Thereof)

Many taxpayers in the U.S. have come to expect a sizable refund check every tax season. To some people who don't prepare their own tax returns, it's a mystery how the refund is calculated.

The idea is really quite simple. After calculating your taxable income, you use the information in the tax tables (from Chapter 1) to determine your total income tax for the year. From this amount, you subtract any credits for which you are eligible. The remainder is then compared to the amount that you actually paid throughout the year (in the form of withholding from your paychecks). If the amount you paid is *more* than your tax, you are entitled to a refund for the difference. If the amount you paid is *less* than your tax, it's time to get out the checkbook.

Withholding: Why It's Done

If you work as an employee, you're certainly aware that a large portion of your wages/salary doesn't actually show up in your paycheck every pay period. Instead, it gets "withheld."

The reason for this withholding is that the federal government wants to be absolutely sure that it gets its money. The government knows that many people have a tendency to spend literally all of the income they receive (if not more). As a result, the government set up the system so that it would get its share before taxpayers would have a chance to spend it.

The amount of your pay that gets withheld is based upon an estimate of how much tax you'll be responsible for paying over the course of the year. (This is why you are required to fill out Form W-4, providing your employer with some tax-related information, when you start a new job.)

Withholding: How It's Calculated

At this point you may be thinking, "OK. Well I just learned that I'm in the __% tax bracket, but it's obvious that my employer is withholding *way* more than that!"

You're probably right. That's because your employer isn't just withholding for federal income tax. They're also withholding for Social Security tax, Medicare tax, and (likely) state income tax.

The Social Security tax is calculated as 6.2% of your earnings, and the Medicare tax is calculated as 1.45% of your earnings. Before you've even begun to pay your income taxes, 7.65% of your income has been withheld.[1]

Your refund is determined by comparing your total income tax (based upon the tax tables from Chapter 1) to the amount that was withheld *for federal income tax*. Assuming that the amount withheld for federal income tax was greater than your income tax for the year, you will receive a refund for the difference.

EXAMPLE: Nick's total taxable income (after subtracting deductions) is $32,000. He is single. Using the table from Chapter 1, we can determine that his federal income tax is $3,649.50.

Over the course of the year, Nick's employer withheld a total of $8,500 from his pay, of which $4,000 went toward federal income tax. His

---

[1] There is a cap on the amount of your earnings that can be subject to the Social Security tax per year. For 2018, that amount is $128,400. In contrast, the Medicare tax applies to all of your earnings. In addition, the rate of the Medicare tax increases from 1.45% to 2.35% for earnings over a certain threshold ($200,000 for single filers, $250,000 for married taxpayers filing jointly).

federal income tax refund will be $350.50 (i.e., $4,000, minus $3,649.50).

Chapter 3 Simple Summary

- Every year, your refund is calculated as the amount withheld for federal income tax, minus your total federal income tax for the year.

- A large portion of the money being withheld from each of your paychecks does not actually go toward federal income tax. Instead, it goes to pay Social Security tax, Medicare tax, and possibly state income tax.

PART TWO

Taxable Income &
Taxable Gains

CHAPTER FOUR

Taxable Income

It's obvious that, in addition to your filing status, the size of your taxable income is the most important factor in determining how much tax you'll be responsible for paying every year. What's not so obvious is that the calculation of your tax is also affected by the *type(s)* of income that you earn. For example, your taxable income could include any of the following types of income, each of which has its own unique tax treatment:

1. Earned income (such as salary, wages, and earnings from self-employment),
2. Interest income,
3. Dividend income,
4. Passive income (such as rental income), and
5. Capital gains (from things such as the sale of stock, which we'll discuss in Chapter 5).

Salary and Wages

For most people, the majority of income comes in the form of salary and wages. Salaries and wages are straightforward in terms of taxes because they are taxable at the normal income tax rates, and they are subject to normal Social Security and Medicare taxes.

If you work as an employee, your salary or wages for each year will be reported to you (and to the IRS) on Form W-2 at the beginning of the following year. The amounts withheld for federal income tax, state income tax, and Social Security and Medicare taxes are also reported on your W-2.

Earnings from Self-Employment

Earnings from self-employment are subject to the same income tax rates as wages or salaries. However, instead of being subject to the normal Social Security and Medicare payroll taxes, self-employment earnings are subject to the self-employment tax.

For employees of a company, a Social Security tax of 6.2% and Medicare tax of 1.45% are withheld from each paycheck. The person's employer is required to pay a matching amount. So the employee is paying 7.65%, and the employer is paying 7.65%, for a grand total of 15.3%. When you're self-employed, there is no employer with whom you get to split the bill, so you end up paying the entire 15.3% as self-employment tax.

In contrast to people who work as employees (who get their income reported to them on a W-2), business owners are responsible for keeping records of how much their businesses make over the course of the year. If, however, you work as an independent contractor, your income—as long as it's over $600—will be reported to you on Form 1099-MISC. (If it's under $600, it won't be reported to you on any form at all, though you're still responsible for reporting it on your tax return.)

Interest Income

Most interest income—such as that from a savings account—is subject to normal income tax rates.[1] It is not, however, subject to Social Security and

---

[1] In addition to ordinary income tax, there is also a 3.8% tax that applies to the lesser of a) your "net investment income" (i.e., interest, dividends, capital gains, royalties, rents, and annuity income) or b) the amount by which your "modified adjusted gross income" exceeds $200,000 ($250,000 if married filing jointly). In this context, modified adjusted gross income refers to your adjusted gross income, plus any tax-exempt foreign earned income.

Medicare taxes. Interest income that you earn will be reported to you on Form 1099-INT.

Some types of interest income are not subject to federal income tax at all. The two most common sources of tax-exempt interest income are bonds issued by state governments and bonds issued by municipalities. One important thing to know is that, while it's not subject to federal income tax, tax-exempt interest income will often be subject to state and local income taxes.

Interest income from U.S. Treasury debt instruments (e.g., Treasury bills or bonds) *is* subject to federal income tax at ordinary income tax rates, but it is exempt from state and local income taxes.

Dividend Income

Dividends—distributions of a corporation's profits to the shareholders—are also taxable. Like interest income, dividend income is not subject to Social Security or Medicare taxes.

Also, dividend income is often subject to lower income tax rates than other types of income. If a dividend meets a list of requirements, it will be referred to as a "qualified dividend." Qualified dividends are taxed at a 0% rate if (for 2018) they fall below $38,600 of taxable income ($77,200 if you're married filing jointly). They are taxed at a

25

15% rate if they fall above the 0% threshold but below $425,800 ($479,000 if married filing jointly). And they are taxed at a 20% rate if they fall above the 15% threshold.

EXAMPLE: Mia is single. She has $5,000 of qualified dividend income in 2018. Excluding her qualified dividends, her taxable income for the year is $36,000.

Her first $2,600 of qualified dividend income is untaxed, because it falls below the $38,600 threshold. The remaining $2,400 of qualified dividends will be taxed at a 15% rate.

Generally, dividends that you receive for shares of stock that you've held for at least the last 60 days will be qualified dividends. Because your Form 1099-DIV (received from your brokerage firm) will indicate what portion of your dividends were qualified dividends, it generally isn't necessary to concern yourself with memorizing all of the specific requirements for a dividend to be a qualified dividend.[1]

---

[1] If, however, you are interested, the requirements are explained in IRS Publication 550, available at: irs.gov/publications/p550/

Passive Income

Passive income includes:

1. All income from trades or businesses in which you do not materially participate, and
2. Rental income, even if you materially participate in the activity (unless you're a real estate professional).

Like interest income, passive income is subject to regular income tax, but it is not subject to payroll taxes or self-employment tax.

The reason passive activities are treated separately from other sources of income is that *losses* from passive activities can only be used to offset income from passive activities. There is, however, an exception to this rule. If you or your spouse actively participate in a rental activity, up to $25,000 of loss from that activity can be used to offset your nonpassive income each year. (Note, however, that this $25,000 amount is reduced by 50% of the amount by which your modified adjusted gross income exceeds $100,000.)

For most landlords, "active participation" is not a terribly difficult standard to meet. Making managerial decisions about the property (e.g., decisions about lease terms, decisions about property repairs, or decisions about which tenants to rent to) qualifies as active participation.

EXAMPLE: Miranda owns a condominium, which she uses as a rental property. She does not actively participate in the activity. In a given year, she has a net loss of $30,000 from the rental property.

If Miranda has passive income from other sources, she can use this $30,000 loss to offset that income. If she does not have any passive income, she cannot claim a deduction for her $30,000 passive loss. Instead, she will carry the loss forward and use it to offset her passive income in future years.

If, however, Miranda had actively participated in the rental activity, she'd be able to deduct $25,000 of the loss from her nonpassive income. The remaining loss would be carried forward for use in future years.

Chapter 4 Simple Summary

Type of Income	Federal Income Tax Rate	Subject to Social Security and Medicare taxes?
Wages/salary	Normal rates	Yes
Self-employment income	Normal rates	Subject to self-employment tax instead
Interest income	Normal rates (assuming it is not tax-exempt interest)	No
Dividend income	Max of 20% (if "qualified dividend")	No
Passive income	Normal rates	No

CHAPTER FIVE

Capital Gains and Losses

When you sell something (such as a share of stock) for more than you paid for it, you're generally going to be taxed on the increase in value. This increase in value is known as a "capital gain."

The amount of gain is calculated as the proceeds received from the sale, minus your "cost basis" in that asset.

What is "Cost Basis"?

In most cases, your cost basis in an asset is simply the amount that you paid for that asset, including any brokerage commissions that you paid on the transaction.[1]

---

[1] If you did not actually *buy* the asset (e.g., gifts, inheritances, etc.) your cost basis will depend upon other factors, explained in Publication 551, available at: irs.gov/publications/p551/

EXAMPLE: Lauren buys fives share of stock for $250, including brokerage commissions. She owns the shares for two years and then sells them for $400. Her cost basis is the amount she paid: $250. Her gain will be calculated as follows:

$400 (proceeds from sale)
– $250 (cost basis)
= $150 (capital gain)

Long-Term Capital Gains vs. Short-Term Capital Gains

The rate of tax charged on a capital gain depends upon whether it was a long-term capital gain (LTCG) or a short-term capital gain (STCG). If the asset in question was held for one year or less, it's a short-term capital gain. If the asset was held for longer than one year, it's a long-term capital gain.[1]

STCGs are taxed at normal income tax rates. In contrast, LTCGs are taxed at the same rates as qualified dividend income. That is, for 2018, LTCGs are taxed at a 0% rate if they fall below $38,600 of taxable income ($77,200 if

---

[1] There are some exceptions to these general rules. For instance, inherited property is considered to be long-term property, even if it has been held for less than one year.

you're married filing jointly). They are taxed at a 15% rate if they fall above the 0% threshold but below $425,800 ($479,000 if married filing jointly). And they are taxed at a 20% rate if they fall above the 15% threshold.

An important takeaway here is that if you're ever considering selling an investment that has increased in value, it's a good idea to think about holding the asset long enough for the capital gain to be considered long-term.

Note that a capital gain occurs only when the asset is sold. This is important because it means that fluctuations in the value of the asset are not considered taxable events.

EXAMPLE: Beth buys ten shares of a company at $25 each. Five years later, Beth still owns the shares, and the price per share has risen to $45. Over the five years, Beth isn't required to pay any tax on the increase in value. She will only have to pay a tax on the LTCG if/when she chooses to sell the shares.

Taxation of Mutual Funds

Mutual funds are collections of a very large quantity of other investments. For instance, a mutual fund may own thousands of different stocks as well as any number of other investments such as bonds or options contracts.

Every year, each mutual fund shareholder is responsible for income tax on her share of the net capital gains realized by the fund over the course of the year. (Each shareholder's portion of the gains will be reported to her annually on Form 1099-DIV sent by the brokerage firm or fund company.)

What makes the situation counterintuitive is that, in any given year, the capital gains realized by the fund could vary significantly from the actual change in value of the shares of the fund.

EXAMPLE: Deborah buys a share of Mutual Fund XYZ on January 1 for $100. By the end of the year, the investments that the fund owns have (on average) decreased in value, and Deborah's share of the mutual fund is now worth $95.

However, during the course of the year, the mutual fund sold only one stock from the portfolio. That stock was sold for a short-term capital gain. Deborah is responsible for paying tax on her share of the capital gain, despite the fact that her share in the mutual fund has decreased in value.

Note how even in years when the value decreases, it's possible that the investors will be responsible for paying taxes on a gain. Of course, the opposite is also true. There can be years when the fund increases in value, but the sales of investments within the fund's portfolio result in a net capital loss. And thus the investors have an increase in the value of their holdings, but they don't have to pay any taxes for the time being.

Fortunately, your basis in the fund is increased each year by an amount equal to your share of the net capital gains realized within the fund's portfolio (unless you choose to have those capital gains distributed to you in cash). This helps to minimize the tax that you'll ultimately have to pay when you sell your shares of the fund.

Capital Gains from Selling Your Home

Selling a home can sometimes result in a very large long-term capital gain. Fortunately, it's likely that you can exclude (that is, not pay tax on) a large portion—or even all—of that gain.

If you meet three requirements, you're allowed to exclude up to $250,000 of gain. The three requirements are as follows:

1. For the two years prior to the date of sale, you did not exclude gain from the sale of another home.

2. During the five years prior to the date of sale, you owned the home for at least two years.
3. During the five years prior to the date of sale, you lived in the home as your main home for at least two years.

To meet the second and third requirements, the two-year time periods do not necessarily have to be made up of 24 consecutive months.

For married couples filing jointly, a $500,000 maximum exclusion is available if both spouses meet the first and third requirements and at least one spouse meets the second requirement.

EXAMPLE: Jason purchased a home on January 1, 2016. He lived there until May 1, 2017 (16 months). He then moved to another city (without selling his original home) and lived there until January 1, 2018. On January 1, 2018 Jason moved back into his original home and lived there until October 1, 2018 (9 months), when he sold the house for a $200,000 gain.

Jason can exclude the gain because he meets all three requirements. The fact that Jason does not have 24 *consecutive* months of using the home as his main home does not prevent him from excluding the gain.

Capital Losses

Of course, things don't always go exactly as planned. When you sell something for less than you paid for it, you incur what is known as a capital loss. Like capital gains, capital losses are characterized as either short-term or long-term, based on whether the holding period of the asset was greater than or less than one year.

Each year, you add up all of your short-term capital losses and deduct them from your short-term capital gains. Then you add up all of your long-term capital losses and deduct them from your long-term capital gains. If the end result is a positive LTCG and a positive STCG, the LTCG will be taxed at a maximum rate of 20%, and the STCG will be taxed at ordinary income tax rates. If the end result is a net capital loss, you can deduct up to $3,000 of it from your ordinary income. The remainder of the capital loss can be carried forward to deduct in future years until it is eventually used in its entirety.

EXAMPLE 1: In a given year, Aaron has:
$5,000 in short-term capital gains,
$3,000 in short-term capital losses,
$4,000 in long-term capital gains, and
$2,500 in long-term capital losses.

For the year, Aaron will have a net STCG of $2,000 ($5,000–$3,000) and a net LTCG of $1,500 ($4,000–$2,500). His STCG will be taxed at his ordinary income tax rate, and his LTCG will be taxed at a maximum rate of 20%.

EXAMPLE 2: In a given year, Sandra has:
$2,000 in short-term capital gains,
$3,500 in short-term capital losses,
$3,000 in long-term capital gains, and
$5,000 in long-term capital losses.

Sandra has a net short-term capital loss of $1,500 and a net long-term capital loss of $2,000. So her total capital loss is $3,500. For this capital loss, she can take a $3,000 deduction against her other income, and she can use the remaining $500 to offset her capital gains next year.

So what happens when you have a net gain in the short-term category and a net loss in the long-term category, or vice versa? You net the two against each other, and the remaining gain or loss is taxed according to its character (that is, short-term or long-term).

EXAMPLE 1: In a given year, Kyle has:
$5,000 net short-term capital gain and
$4,000 net long-term capital loss.

Kyle will subtract his LTCL from his STCG, leaving him with a STCG of $1,000. This will be taxed according to his ordinary income tax bracket.

EXAMPLE 2: In a given year, Christopher has:
$3,000 net short-term capital loss and
$6,000 net long-term capital gain.

Christopher will subtract his STCL from his LTCG, leaving him with a LTCG of $3,000. This will be taxed at a maximum rate of 20%.

EXAMPLE 3: In a given year, Jeremy has:
$2,000 net short-term capital gain and
$3,000 net long-term capital loss.

Jeremy will subtract his LTCL from his STCG, leaving him with a $1,000 LTCL. Because this is below the $3,000 threshold, he can deduct the entire $1,000 loss from his ordinary income.

EXAMPLE 4: In a given year, Jessica has:
$2,000 net long-term capital gain and
$4,000 net short-term capital loss.

Jessica will subtract her STCL from her LTCG, leaving her with a $2,000 STCL. Because this is below the $3,000 threshold, she can deduct the entire $2,000 loss from her ordinary income.

Chapter 5 Simple Summary

- If an asset is held for one year or less, then sold for a gain, the short-term capital gain will be taxed at ordinary income tax rates.

- If an asset is held for more than one year, then sold for a gain, the long-term capital gain will be taxed at a maximum rate of 20%.

- If you have a net capital loss for the year, you can subtract up to $3,000 of that loss from your ordinary income. The remainder of the loss can be carried forward to offset income in future years.

- Mutual fund shareholders have to pay taxes each year as a result of the net gains realized by the fund. This is unique in that taxes have to be paid before the asset (i.e., the mutual fund) is sold.

- If you sell your home for a gain, and you meet certain requirements, you may be eligible to exclude up to $250,000 of the gain ($500,000 if married filing jointly).

PART THREE

Important Deductions
and Credits

CHAPTER SIX

Saving for Retirement: IRAs and 401(k)s

IRAs are simply investment accounts with some additional benefits and restrictions tacked on. The main benefit of contributing money to a traditional IRA is that when you do, you get an above the line deduction for the amount of the contribution.

After money has been contributed to a traditional IRA, you can invest it in (almost) anything you'd like: stocks, bonds, mutual funds, CDs, etc. The money then grows tax-free while it remains in the account. However, when you do eventually take money out of the account, the amount of the withdrawal is taxable as income.

Because of this tax-deduction-now, taxable-withdrawals-later structure, traditional IRAs are sometimes referred to as "tax-deferred" investment accounts. There are two primary advantages to tax-deferred investing.

The first advantage is the result of good timing. Assuming you make your contributions during your pre-retirement years, you get your deductions in years while your income is at a high point, thus maximizing the value of the deduction. Then, when you begin to make withdrawals during retirement, you'll be taxed on the withdrawal, but by then you'll likely be in a lower tax bracket because you're no longer working.

The second benefit to tax-deferred investing is that your money can grow more quickly when it's not being taxed on its growth along the way. Even when you account for the fact that it will be taxable when you withdraw it, you still (usually) come out with more after-tax money than you would if you were simply investing in a taxable investment account.

The Rules for Investing in an IRA

In exchange for granting you a tax deduction for investing in a traditional IRA, the government requires you to jump through a few hoops. There are restrictions on both the deduction that you get for investing via a traditional IRA and on your ability to withdraw money from your IRA.

First, as of 2018, the annual limit for IRA contributions is the lesser of:

- $5,500 (unless you're 50 or older, in which case you're allowed to contribute up to $6,500), or
- Your taxable compensation for the year.[1]

Second, if your income reaches a certain level, you may no longer qualify to receive a deduction for the amount that you contribute to a traditional IRA. However, even if you do reach this point, you are still allowed to make contributions, and you will not be taxed on the growth until you withdraw the money from the account.

The income limits for being able to receive a deduction for traditional IRA contributions only come into play if either you or your spouse is covered by a retirement plan at work (such as a 401(k), which we'll discuss shortly).

If you are covered by a retirement plan at work, your deduction for a traditional IRA contribution will begin to decrease (and eventually

---

[1] If you're married filing jointly, you can count your spouse's taxable compensation for the purpose of determining this limit. That is, you and your spouse's *combined* IRA contributions are limited to your *combined* taxable compensation for the year.

disappear entirely) as your modified adjusted gross income (MAGI)[1] for 2018 surpasses:

- $63,000 for single taxpayers, and
- $101,000 for married taxpayers filing jointly.

If your spouse is covered by a retirement plan at work, but you are not, your deduction for a traditional IRA contribution begins to be phased out once your joint modified adjusted gross income passes $189,000 for 2018.

Restrictions on IRA Distributions

Congress's goal when originally creating the laws that allow for IRAs was to encourage people to save for retirement, so they implemented some restrictions regarding taking money out of a traditional IRA.

The most notable restriction is that any withdrawals (technically referred to as "IRA distributions") that you take before age 59½ will be subject to a 10% tax, in addition to being subject to normal income taxes.

---

[1] In this context, your MAGI is your adjusted gross income with a few specific deductions added back in. See IRS Publication 590-A for more info: irs.gov/publications/p590a/

There are several exceptions to the 59½ rule, however. A distribution will not be subject to the additional 10% tax if:

- You are disabled;
- You are deceased and the distribution was made to your beneficiary or to your estate;
- The distribution does not exceed the amount that you're able to claim as an itemized deduction for medical expenses for the year (more on this deduction in Chapter 7);
- You are unemployed, you receive at least 12 consecutive weeks of unemployment compensation, and the distribution is used to pay for health insurance for yourself, your spouse, or your dependents;
- The distribution does not exceed your qualified higher education costs for the year (e.g., college expenses for yourself, your spouse, your child, or grandchild); or
- The distribution is used to buy or build your first home. (Note: Only the first $10,000 of distributions for this purpose will be free from the additional 10% tax.)

Roth IRAs: Tax-Free Distributions

In addition to the traditional IRA, there is an alternative type of IRA known as the Roth IRA.

The biggest difference between a traditional IRA and a Roth IRA is that you do *not* get a deduction for contributions to a Roth IRA. Instead, as long as you meet certain requirements, when you take money out of your Roth IRA, it will be tax-free. Even the earnings on your contributions come out free of tax.

Restrictions on Roth IRAs

As you'd expect, there are rules and restrictions relating to investing via a Roth IRA. First, Roth IRAs share a combined contribution limit with traditional IRAs. That is, for 2018, your total contributions to Roth and/or traditional IRAs are limited to the lesser of:

- $5,500 ($6,500 if you're age 50 or over), or
- The total of your taxable compensation for the year.

In addition, your eligibility to contribute to a Roth IRA is reduced (and eventually eliminated) as your income increases:

- For 2018, for single taxpayers and taxpayers filing as head of household, the amount you can contribute to a Roth IRA begins to decrease as your modified adjusted gross income surpasses $120,000. Once your MAGI reaches $135,000, you can no longer contribute to a Roth IRA.

- For 2018, for married taxpayers filing jointly, the amount you can contribute to a Roth IRA begins to decrease as your modified adjusted gross income surpasses $189,000. Once your MAGI reaches $199,000, you can no longer contribute to a Roth IRA.

Note that the income limits are much higher for Roth IRAs than they are for traditional IRA deductions.

With a Roth IRA, at any point in time, you can withdraw *contributions* free from tax and penalty. However, distributions of *earnings* (e.g., interest earned on your contributions) from a Roth IRA may be subject to income tax and a 10% additional tax unless they meet certain requirements. In order for a distribution of earnings to be free from income tax and the additional 10% tax, the distribution must be made at least 5 years after the beginning of the year in which you made your first contribution to a Roth IRA, and one of the following requirements must be met:

- You are 59½ or older,
- You are disabled,

- You have died and the distribution is being made to your estate or to the beneficiary of the IRA, or
- The distribution is used to buy or build your first home. (These "qualified first-time homebuyer" distributions are limited to $10,000.)

Which Type of IRA is Better for Me?

In most cases, when it comes to choosing between a traditional IRA and a Roth IRA, the most important factor in the decision is how your current marginal tax rate compares to the marginal tax rate you expect to face during retirement.[1]

EXAMPLE 1: Pam works as an upper-level manager at a graphic design firm. Her employer does not currently offer a retirement plan. She is unmarried and earns $130,000 annually.

Given the high probability that Pam will be in a lower tax bracket once she retires than she is in at the moment, it makes sense for her to con-

---

[1] One important exception: If there's a meaningful chance that you'll need this money prior to retirement age, Roth IRAs have a big advantage in that you can take contributions back out of the account without having to pay tax or penalty.

tribute to a traditional IRA. The value of receiving a deduction now, while she's in the 24% tax bracket, likely outweighs the value of being able to take tax-free distributions once she's retired.

EXAMPLE 2: Laurie is a college student who works full-time in the summer and part-time throughout the school year. Laurie expects to earn a total of $14,000 this year.

A Roth IRA is almost certainly the best option for Laurie. At the moment, she's only in the 10% tax bracket, so the value of a deduction from a traditional IRA contribution isn't that great. The ability to grow her money (and eventually withdraw it) free of tax in a Roth IRA is much more valuable.

EXAMPLE 3: Carlos is currently unmarried, and he earns $100,000 per year. His employer offers a 401(k) plan to which he can contribute. After making the maximum contribution to his 401(k) (discussed in the next section), Carlos still wants to invest more money for retirement.

Despite the fact that a contribution to a traditional IRA would be appealing, he has little choice here. Because he has a retirement plan at work, and because of his income level, he is ineligible for a deduction for a traditional IRA contribution. As a result, his best choice is probably a Roth IRA.

If Carlos made, for example, $200,000 annually, he would be unable to contribute to a Roth IRA, and his only IRA option would be to make nondeductible contributions to a traditional IRA.

401(k) Plans

A 401(k) plan is a deferred compensation plan through which an employee can choose to have some of her wages/salary deposited into a tax-deferred investment account. In other words, having a 401(k) is much like having a traditional IRA through your work.[1] There are, however, several noteworthy differences between 401(k) accounts and IRAs.

Investing via a 401(k) Account

The first and foremost difference is that 401(k) accounts have much higher contribution limits than IRAs. If you are under age 50, your contribution limit is $18,500 for 2018. If you are 50 or over, your contribution limit for 2018 is $24,500.

---

[1] 403(b) and 457(b) plans are tax-deferred plans (often offered by non-profit or governmental employers) that work similarly (though not identically) to 401(k) plans.

A second, potentially important difference is that in a 401(k), your investment options will be limited to a pre-selected group of mutual funds. This isn't necessarily going to be a problem, but it's possible that you'll be stuck with unappealing, high-cost mutual funds. (It's been shown time and again that mutual funds with low expense ratios tend to outperform mutual funds with higher expense ratios.)

A third difference deals with accessing your money. With an IRA (whether Roth or traditional), you can take your money out of the account at any time. The only question is whether the distribution will be taxable and/or subject to the 10% additional tax. In contrast, with a 401(k) plan, you might not be able to take distributions from the account at all until you have left the employer in question. (Some plans provide an option for financial hardship distributions, loans from the plan, or "in-service" distributions for employees age 59½ or over.)

401(k) Distributions

Like IRA distributions, distributions from a 401(k) will be subject to an additional 10% tax if you are under age 59½. However, the list of exceptions to the 59½ rule is different with 401(k) accounts than it is with IRAs. The most important differences are that:

- 401(k) distributions for a first time home purchase are not granted an exemption from the additional 10% tax,
- 401(k) distributions for paying higher education expenses are not granted an exemption from the additional 10% tax, and
- 401(k) distributions made to an employee after separation from service—if the separation occurred during or after the calendar year in which the employee reached age 55—*are* exempt from the additional 10% tax.

401(k) Rollovers

When you leave your job, you can transfer your 401(k) into either a traditional IRA or a 401(k) with your new employer. This nontaxable transfer is known as a 401(k) rollover. In many cases, a rollover to an IRA is a wise idea, because it will provide access to a broader range of investment options and will allow you to escape from the administrative fees charged by many 401(k) plans.

Roth 401(k) Accounts

Today, many employers offer the option to make Roth contributions to the company's 401(k) plan. Roth 401(k) accounts share a combined contribution limit with regular 401(k) accounts. That is, the *total* amount you can contribute is limited to $18,500 for 2018 ($24,500 if you're 50 or older).

A Roth 401(k) functions much like a normal 401(k), with two primary differences. First, contributions to a Roth 401(k) do not reduce your taxable income. Second, distributions from a Roth 401(k) are not subject to income tax, provided that they occur:

1. After you have reached age 59½ (or died or become disabled), and
2. At least 5 years after the first day of the calendar year in which you first made a Roth contribution to the plan.

If you take any distributions from a Roth 401(k) prior to satisfying those two requirements, the portion of the distribution that represents earnings (rather than contributions you made to the account) will be taxable as income and potentially subject to a 10% additional tax.

Chapter 6 Simple Summary

- If your income is below a certain limit, you can claim an above the line deduction for contributions to a traditional IRA.

- As long as you meet certain requirements, distributions from a Roth IRA are tax-free. However, there are income limits that may reduce or eliminate your ability to contribute to a Roth IRA.

- In many cases, if you withdraw money from your IRA prior to age 59½, the withdrawal will be subject to an extra 10% tax.

- Investing in a 401(k) is akin to investing in a traditional IRA with a very high contribution limit.

- 401(k) distributions taken prior to age 59½ are generally subject to an extra 10% tax. As with IRAs, there are some exceptions.

- A Roth 401(k) is essentially a hybrid of a Roth IRA and a regular 401(k) account, providing high contribution limits and the opportunity for tax-free distributions.

CHAPTER SEVEN

Other Important Deductions

Rather than try to discuss every obscure deduction that exists, we'll cover a handful of deductions that you're most likely be able to use at some point.

Health Savings Accounts

Health Savings Accounts (HSAs) are akin to IRAs for medical expenses. When you contribute to an HSA, you get an above the line deduction for the amount of the contribution. While money remains in the account, it can grow tax-free. And the best part is that distributions from the account are tax-free as well, if the money is used to pay for qualified medical expenses. In other words, when used for medical expenses, HSAs offer the best part of traditional IRAs (deductible contributions) *and* the best part of Roth IRAs (tax-free distributions).

Most expenses for medical care and prescription drugs (as well as non-prescription insulin) for yourself, your spouse, or your dependent will count as qualified medical expenses. Health insurance premiums, however, do not usually count as a qualified medical expense. Publication 969 has more details on what does and doesn't qualify.[1]

If a distribution from your HSA is not used for qualified medical expenses, the distribution will be taxable and (unless you are deceased, disabled, or at least age 65) subject to an additional 20% tax.

In order to qualify to contribute to an HSA, you must be enrolled in a "high deductible health plan." For a health insurance plan to qualify as an HDHP, it must have a deductible of at least (for 2018) $1,350 for self-only coverage or $2,700 for family coverage. In addition, the plan must have an out-of-pocket maximum of no more than (for 2018) $6,650 for self-only coverage or $13,300 for family coverage.

For 2018, if you are covered by a high deductible health plan for the entire year, the health savings account contribution limit is $3,450 if you have self-only coverage under that plan or

---

[1] Available at: irs.gov/publications/p969/

$6,900 if you have family coverage under that plan. If you are only covered by the plan for a portion of the year, your contribution limit will be reduced (unless you are covered as of the first day of the last month of the year, in which case you are considered to be covered for the entire year).

Pass-Through Business Income Deduction

If you have income from a "pass-through" business (i.e., profit from a sole proprietorship, partnership, S-corporation, or an LLC taxed as any of the above), you likely qualify for a related deduction.

If your taxable income is under a certain threshold amount, the deduction is calculated as 20% of the pass-through income from your business(es), but it cannot be greater than 20% of your taxable income excluding net capital gains. The threshold amounts for 2018 are $315,000 if you are married filling jointly or $157,500 if you are single, head of household, or married filing separately.

If your taxable income exceeds the threshold, the calculation of the deduction becomes quite a bit more complicated, as three additional limitations come into play. (If your income is in this higher range, it's definitely worth speaking with a tax professional to discuss these limitations and related tax planning opportunities.)[1]

The deduction for pass-through business income is somewhat unique. It is not considered an "above the line" deduction because it is subtracted *after* adjusted gross income is calculated. But it is also not an itemized deduction; that is, you can claim it as well as the standard deduction in a given year.

Home Mortgage Interest

In most cases, if you own a home, you can deduct (as an itemized/below the line deduction) any interest that you pay on your mortgage. As you'd expect, there are some requirements that must be met in order to take the deduction.

First, the mortgage must be "secured debt." All this means is that your home must be used as collateral for the loan. Of course, a typical homeowner's mortgage meets this requirement.

Second, the loan must be "acquisition indebtedness." That is, the proceeds from the mortgage must have been used to purchase, build, or

---

[1] For more information about these limitations, see the following article:

obliviousinvestor.com/pass-through-income-deduction/

substantially improve your primary home or qualifying second home.

Finally, if the loan was taken out after 12/15/17, only interest on the first $750,000 of the loan ($375,000 if you're married filing separately) can be deducted. A $1,000,000 limit ($500,000 if married filing separately) applies for loans taken out on 12/15/17 or earlier.

In a given year, in order to claim the itemized deduction for home mortgage interest paid on a *second* home, you must either:

- Not rent the home out to anyone else, or
- Live in the home for (at least) the greater of 14 days or 10% of the number of days that the home is rented out at fair rental value.

If the home does not satisfy either of the above requirements, it will be considered rental property. While this will preclude claiming an itemized deduction for home mortgage interest, you may be able to claim the interest as a rental expense. (See the discussion of passive income in Chapter 4.)

Deduction for State and Local Taxes

Each year, you can claim an itemized deduction for many of the state and local taxes you paid over the course of the year, including:

- Real estate taxes,
- Personal property taxes, and
- State and local income taxes *or* state and local sales taxes (your choice).

Beginning in 2018, the deduction for state and local taxes is limited to $10,000 per year ($5,000 if married filling separately).

Charitable Contributions

As you probably know if you've ever been solicited for a donation, you're entitled to an itemized deduction for contributions that you make to charitable organizations. As you'd expect, there are some restrictions.

For example, if you make a contribution from which you'll also receive some benefit, you're only allowed to take a deduction for the amount by which the contribution exceeds the fair market value of the benefit that you receive.

EXAMPLE: Steve pays $100 for a ticket to a fund-raiser dinner at his church. The value of the dinner is approximately $20. Steve can only deduct $80 for the contribution.

Donating Property

Generally, when you donate property to a qualified organization, you're entitled to a deduction equal to the fair market value of the property.

However, if you are donating property that would trigger a short-term capital gain (or ordinary income) if you sold it, your deduction is limited to your basis in the property.

EXAMPLE: Liliana owns shares of stock that she purchased 18 months ago for a total of $4,000. The shares are currently worth $6,000. If she donates them to a qualified organization, she's entitled to a deduction for their fair market value ($6,000).[1]

If, however, she had only owned the shares for 6 months (such that a sale of them would cause a short-term capital gain), she would only be entitled to a $4,000 deduction.

---

[1] As you can see from this example, donating appreciated long-term capital gain property is often more tax-efficient than simply writing a check to the charity of your choice, because in addition to getting a deduction for the current value of the property, you get to avoid paying tax on the accumulated gain.

Donating Services

Services donated to qualified organizations are *not* deductible. However, if you incur any expenses in the course of providing your donated services, you may claim a deduction for those expenses.

EXAMPLE: Barrie is a freelance web designer. He decides to donate his services to a local church, creating a website for them for which he would ordinarily charge $1,000. In order to create the website, he spends $90 on a template for his web design software. Barrie cannot deduct the value of his services, but he can deduct the $90 spent on the template.

Recordkeeping for Charitable Contributions

For cash contributions of less than $250, all you're required to keep as proof is a canceled check, a bank statement, or a credit card statement indicating the amount and date of the contribution as well as the name of the organization.[1]

For cash contributions of $250 or more, you will need to get some form of written acknowl-

---

[1] In this instance, "cash contributions" refers to contributions made by cash, check, or credit/debit card.

edgement of the contribution from the organization to which you made the donation. The acknowledgement must:

- State the amount of cash you donated,
- State the date of the donation, and
- State an estimate of the value (if any) of any goods or services that you received in exchange for the contribution.

For noncash contributions of less than $250, you'll need to keep a receipt or record indicating:

- The name of the organization,
- The date and location of the contribution, and
- A "reasonably detailed" description of the property contributed.

For noncash contributions between $250 and $500, you will need the same records as for contributions below $250, plus an acknowledgement of the donation from the recipient organization. As with cash contributions, the acknowledgement must state the value (if any) of any goods or services that you received in exchange for your donation.

For noncash contributions between $500 and $5,000, you will need the same records as for contributions between $250 and $500. You will also need to keep records of the following information:

- How you originally obtained the property (purchase, gift, etc.),
- The approximate date that you obtained the property, and
- Your cost basis in the property.

Noncash contributions of greater than $5,000 require all of the same records, plus a written appraisal of the property, provided by a qualified appraiser.

Limit on Charitable Contribution Deductions

One final point of note about deductions for charitable contributions is that there's a limitation on the maximum deduction you are allowed. What the limit is depends upon what type of organizations you're contributing to, as well as what type of property you're contributing.

Luckily, these limitations don't affect most taxpayers, as they don't kick in until your charitable contributions exceed 20% of your adjusted gross income.[1]

Deduction for Medical Expenses

A deduction is allowed for unreimbursed medical expenses. However, many taxpayers do not get to use this deduction as a result of two factors. First, it's an itemized deduction. Second, the amount of the deduction is reduced by 10% of your adjusted gross income (7.5% for 2017 and 2018). In other words, the deduction is only helpful if (and to the extent that) your medical expenses exceed 10% of your AGI.

When calculating your deduction for medical expenses, you can include medical and dental expenses paid for yourself, your spouse, and your dependents. Deductible expenses include health and dental insurance premiums, as well as payments made for the cure, prevention, diagnosis, mitigation, or treatment of disease. With the exception of insulin, only prescription drugs can be included in the deduction.

---

[1] For more information about these limitations, see IRS Publication 526 at: irs.gov/publications/p526/

Chapter 7 Simple Summary

- Health savings accounts are a tax-efficient way to save for medical expenses. To qualify to contribute to an HSA, you must be enrolled in a high deductible health plan.

- If you have pass-through income from a business, you may be eligible for a deduction related to that income.

- If you own a home, you are likely entitled to an itemized deduction for interest that you pay on your mortgage.

- You can claim an itemized deduction (up to $10,000 each year) for certain state and local taxes paid over the course of the year.

- Donations of cash or property to charitable organizations can be taken as itemized deductions.

- An itemized deduction is allowed for medical expenses to the extent that they exceed 10% of your adjusted gross income (7.5% for 2017 and 2018).

CHAPTER EIGHT

Important Credits

As we did with deductions, rather than attempt to cover every single credit, let's just take a look at those that are most commonly available. Remember, credits are especially valuable in that they reduce your tax dollar for dollar, as opposed to deductions, which reduce your taxable income. That is, a credit of a given amount is worth more to you than a deduction of the same amount.

Earned Income Credit

The earned income credit is a tax break for working people whom Congress has determined to be lower-income taxpayers.

In 2018, to be able to claim the credit, you must meet one of the following requirements:

- You have three or more qualifying children and you earn less than $49,298 ($54,998 if married filing jointly),
- You have two qualifying children and you earn less than $45,898 ($51,598 if married filing jointly),
- You have one qualifying child and you earn less than $40,402 ($46,102 if married filing jointly), or
- You do not have a qualifying child and you earn less than $15,310 ($21,000 if married filing jointly).

You aren't responsible for calculating the amount of the credit, as the IRS will do it for you. If, however, you want to know ahead of time how much your credit will be, you can check the earned income credit worksheet and table in the instructions to Form 1040.[1] You'll see that the credit varies as a function of both:

- The number of qualifying children you have, and
- Your earned income or adjusted gross income, depending on circumstances.

---

[1] Available at irs.gov/pub/irs-pdf/i1040.pdf

Child (or Dependent) Tax Credit

The child tax credit is a credit of up to $2,000 per year for each qualifying child. In order to count as a qualifying child, the child must:

- Be under age 17 at the end of the year;
- Live with you for more than half of the year;
- Not provide half of his/her own support; and
- Be your child, stepchild, foster child, sibling, stepsibling, half sibling, or a descendant of any of the above.

If there is somebody else who does not meet the tests to be your qualifying child (e.g., because he/she is your parent rather than your child), but you provide more than half of this person's support and his/her gross income for the year is less than (for 2018) $4,150, you may be eligible for a $500 credit for such person.

The total amount of your child tax credit is reduced if your modified adjusted gross income exceeds $200,000 ($400,000 if married filing jointly).

Child and Dependent Care Credit

If, during the course of the year, you pay somebody to care for your child (or other dependent) so that you (and your spouse, if you're married) can work, you're likely eligible for the child and dependent care credit. In order to claim the credit you must:

- Have earned income during the year. (If you're married, your spouse must also have earned income.)
- Pay child care or dependent care expenses so that you (and your spouse, if married) can work or look for work.
- Make the payments to somebody who cannot be claimed as your dependent. (For example, paying your 14-year-old son to watch your 8-year-old daughter doesn't count.)
- Identify the care provider on your tax return.
- File a joint return with your spouse if you're married.

Also, the payments cannot be made to the parent of the child for whom the care is being provided.

The amount of the credit is a percentage of the expenses paid. The percentage varies from 20% to 35%, depending on your income. (The more you make, the lower the percentage.) A table with the applicable percentage at each income level can be found in IRS Publication 503.[1]

The amount of expenses that you use to calculate the credit is limited in two ways. First, it's limited to your earned income during the course of the year. (If you're married, it's limited to the lesser of your earned income or your spouse's earned income.) Second, it's limited to $3,000 for one child or dependent, or $6,000 for two or more children or dependents.

Retirement Savings Contribution Credit

The retirement savings contribution credit is a credit available to you if you are not a full-time student, you are not somebody else's dependent, and you contributed to either an IRA (of any kind) or a retirement plan at work, such as a 401(k). To claim this credit, your adjusted gross income for 2018 must be less than:

- $63,000 if married filing jointly,
- $47,250 if filing as head of household, or
- $31,500 if single or married filing separately.

---

[1] Available at irs.gov/publications/p503/

Each year, the amount of the credit can be 10%, 20%, or 50% of the first $2,000 of contributions that you make to your retirement accounts over the course of the year. Form 8880 has a table showing what percentage to use for calculating your credit.[1] (The higher your income, the lower the percentage.) For married couples filing jointly, the credit is calculated based on the first $2,000 of contributions to *each* spouse's retirement accounts.

EXAMPLE: Lee is single, and his adjusted gross income for 2018 is $26,000. During the year he contributes $1,500 to a Roth IRA. Form 8880 shows that at $26,000, a single person's credit is equal to 10% of his eligible retirement account contributions. Therefore, Lee's retirement savings contribution credit will be $150 for 2018.

What makes the retirement savings contribution credit so great is that it rewards you for doing something that is beneficial to do anyway. If you qualify for the credit, you're essentially getting an extra 10%-50% return on your money, in addition to whatever it earns on its own.

---

[1] Available at irs.gov/pub/irs-pdf/f8880.pdf

Premium Tax Credit

If you purchase health insurance on one of the exchanges created by the Affordable Care Act, you may qualify for the premium tax credit. To be eligible for the credit, your "household income" must be between 100% and 400% of the federal poverty level.[1] For example, for calculating the credit in 2018, 400% of the federal poverty level would be $48,240 for a family of one, or $64,960 for a family of two.

In addition to the income requirement, you must meet a few other requirements in order to qualify for the premium tax credit:

- If you're married, you must file a joint return,
- You must not be somebody else's dependent, and
- You must not be eligible for "minimum essential coverage" through any other source

---

[1] Your "household income" is defined as your adjusted gross income (i.e., total income, minus above the line deductions), plus tax-exempt foreign-earned income, tax-exempt interest income, and tax-exempt Social Security benefits—plus all of the same types of income for anybody else who would be counted in the household for the purposes of this credit (i.e., your spouse and dependents).

(e.g., your employer, Medicare, Medicaid, etc.). There is, however, an exception to this requirement for people who have employer coverage that is deemed "unaffordable."

One thing that is unique about the premium tax credit is that it can be claimed in advance. The applications for coverage ask for an estimate of your annual income, and if your estimate is such that it would make you eligible for a credit, you can take that credit in advance in the form of lower monthly insurance premiums.

But, when it comes time to file your tax return for the year (e.g., April 2019 for your 2018 return), you effectively "settle up." If your income ends up being lower than you had estimated, and you are therefore eligible for a larger credit than you received in advance, you can receive the remainder of the credit when you file your return. Conversely, if your income ended up being higher than you had estimated, you have to pay back the excess credit that you received in advance. (There are, however, some limitations on the amount you would have to pay back.)

Environmental Credits

If you add solar panels or solar hot water heaters to your home, you may qualify for a credit, calculated as 30% of the cost of the improvement. (This percentage drops to 26% for 2020 and 22% for 2021. The credit expires in 2022.) For more information about this credit, see the instructions to Form 5695.[1]

If you purchase a plug-in electric drive vehicle (e.g. a Chevrolet Volt), you may qualify for a credit ranging from $2,500 to $7,500. To qualify, the vehicle must not be pre-owned, it must have four or more wheels, it must have a gross vehicle weight rating of less than 14,000 pounds, and it must be propelled to a significant extent by a battery with a capacity of at least four kilowatt hours, which can be recharged from an external source of electricity. For more information about the plug-in electric drive vehicle credit, see the instructions to Form 8936.[2]

---

[1] Available at irs.gov/pub/irs-pdf/f5695.pdf
[2] Available at irs.gov/pub/irs-pdf/f8936.pdf

Chapter 8 Simple Summary

- If you work during 2018, and your earned income is less than $49,298 ($54,998 if married filing jointly), you may be eligible for the earned income credit.

- If you have dependent children, you may qualify for the child tax credit and possibly the child and dependent care credit as well.

- If you contribute to an IRA or retirement plan at work, and your 2018 adjusted gross income is below $31,500 ($63,000 if married filing jointly), you may qualify for the retirement savings contribution credit.

- If you purchase health insurance on one of the exchanges created by the Affordable Care Act, you may qualify for the premium tax credit.

- If you purchase solar panels or a solar water heater for your home or purchase a new plug-in electric drive vehicle, you may qualify for a credit to offset a part of the cost.

CHAPTER NINE

Tax Breaks for Education Expenses

Given that the tax law is (usually) set up to reward things that Congress has decided are beneficial to our country, it's no surprise that there are tax breaks available to people paying for higher education expenses.

Education Credits

If you pay higher education expenses for yourself, your spouse, or your dependent, you may be entitled to one (or both) of two credits: the Lifetime Learning Credit or the American Opportunity Credit.

Lifetime Learning Credit

The Lifetime Learning Credit may be available to you if you pay postsecondary education expenses for a student. The credit is calculated as 20% of the first $10,000 of qualified education expenses that you pay in a given year. (Note that this means that the maximum credit per tax return is $2,000.)

Your eligibility to claim the Lifetime Learning Credit begins to decrease as your modified adjusted gross income exceeds $57,000 for 2018 ($114,000 if married filing jointly). Once your MAGI reaches $67,000 ($134,000 if married filing jointly), you'll no longer be eligible to use the credit.

There is no limit to the number of years that the Lifetime Learning Credit can be used for a given student.

In order to qualify for the Lifetime Learning Credit, the expenses must be paid to a university, college, vocational school, or other postsecondary educational institution. Eligible expenses include tuition, fees, and other course-related expenses that are required to be paid *to the institution* as a condition for enrollment or attendance. The course must be part of a postsecondary degree program or taken by the student to acquire or improve job skills.

EXAMPLE: Jack is attending school to be a filmmaker. In addition to his tuition, he's required to pay $500 per semester for use of the school's film studio. Because he is required to pay the $500 to the school in order to attend classes, the expense can be included as a qualifying education expense.

EXAMPLE: Lee is attending school for a degree in Spanish. Each semester, he is required to buy several textbooks and DVDs to use for his courses. However, because his school doesn't require him to buy the materials from the school—he could buy them online on Amazon, for instance—the cost does not count as a qualifying education expense.

Two more points of note about qualifying expenses:

1. Room and board does not count as a qualifying education expense.
2. It doesn't matter whether or not the money used to pay the expenses was obtained with a loan.

American Opportunity Credit

The American Opportunity Credit is available for students who are in their first four years of postsecondary education and who are enrolled at least "half-time." The amount of the credit is the sum of the first $2,000 of qualified education expenses paid for the student, plus 25% of the next $2,000 of qualified expenses. (Note that this means that the maximum credit per student is $2,500.)

Your eligibility to claim the American Opportunity Credit begins to decrease as your modified adjusted gross income exceeds $80,000 ($160,000 if married filing jointly). Once your MAGI reaches $90,000 ($180,000 if married filing jointly), you'll no longer be eligible to use the credit.

In addition to the expenses that can be used when calculating the Lifetime Learning Credit, expenditures for "course materials" can be used for purposes of calculating the American Opportunity Credit. "Course materials" includes books and supplies needed for a course, whether or not the materials are purchased from the educational institution as a condition of enrollment or attendance.

How the Credits Work Together

For a given student, you can claim *either* the Lifetime Learning Credit *or* the American Opportunity Credit in a given year, not both.

EXAMPLE: Katie and Alex are siblings. Alex is a freshman in college, and Katie is a senior (in her fifth year of college). With the help of some student loans, their family spends $20,000 for tuition for each of them for the year.

The family should probably claim the American Opportunity Credit for Alex, because it will allow for a credit of $2,500, as opposed to the $2,000 that would be allowed via the Lifetime Learning Credit. Also, by *not* using the Lifetime Learning Credit for Alex, the family can still use the Lifetime Learning Credit for Katie. (Katie is ineligible for the American Opportunity Credit, because she is in her fifth year of college.) In total, the family will be able to claim $4,500 of education-related credits.

Student Loan Interest Deduction

If you pay interest on student loans, you may be able to deduct that interest (up to $2,500 per year) as an above the line deduction. In order to qualify:

1. The loan must be taken out solely to pay for qualified higher education expenses,
2. You (and your spouse, if you're married) must not be a dependent of anybody else, and
3. If married, you must file jointly.

The $2,500 limit for the deduction is reduced as your modified adjusted gross income exceeds (for 2018) $65,000 ($135,000 if married filing jointly). Once your modified adjusted gross income reaches $80,000 ($165,000 if married filing jointly), you will no longer be eligible for the deduction.

Chapter 9 Simple Summary

- If you pay postsecondary education expenses for yourself, your spouse, or your dependent, you may be eligible for the Lifetime Learning Credit (of up to $2,000). Only one Lifetime Learning Credit can be claimed per tax return per year.

- If you pay postsecondary education expenses for yourself, your spouse, or a dependent, you may be eligible to claim the American Opportunity Credit (of up to $2,500 per student).

- For a given student's expenses each year, you can use *either* the American Opportunity Credit *or* the Lifetime Learning Credit, not both.

- If you pay student loan interest, you may qualify for an above the line deduction for the amount of interest paid, up to $2,500.

PART FOUR

Other Important Things to Know

CHAPTER TEN

Tax Forms

One of the more intimidating aspects of taxation in the United States is the seemingly endless list of tax forms. Just looking at all the tiny print and numerous boxes to be filled in on each form can be enough to make an uninitiated taxpayer dizzy.

The good news is that the situation is really far less complicated than it appears. Most likely, you'll only have to fill out a handful of forms for your annual tax return (Form 1040, and a couple of accompanying schedules or forms). Many people don't even have it that bad: Every year, millions of taxpayers are eligible to file Form 1040EZ (an easier version of Form 1040 that only takes a few minutes to prepare).

What further simplifies the situation is that each of the forms comes with a set of line-by-line instructions that is fairly easy to understand.

When done carefully and one step at a time, many tax forms can be prepared successfully by somebody with only a basic understanding of taxation.

Form 1040

Form 1040 is the primary form for an individual's income tax return.[1] In other words, it's the one single form that you're going to be filing every year, almost regardless of circumstances. As a result, it makes sense to take a little time to become familiar with it.

Form 1040 is only two pages long, and the first part of the form is simply filling in information like your name, address, filing status, etc.

In the next section you list each of your different sources (and amounts) of income: wages, interest, dividends, business income, etc. You then add up all of your income sources to arrive at your "total income."

The next section is where you enter all of your above the line deductions (such as traditional IRA contributions or student loan interest). You then subtract the total of your above the line deductions from your total income to arrive at your adjusted gross income. Next, you subtract either your standard deduction or the sum of your

---

[1] Available at irs.gov/pub/irs-pdf/f1040.pdf

itemized deductions to arrive at your taxable income.

Finally, you use your taxable income to determine your total income tax. From this number, subtract any credits for which you're eligible, and then compare the remainder to the amount that was withheld from your paychecks over the course of the year for federal income taxes. This will show whether you have a refund coming or if it's time to write a check to the United States Treasury.

As you can see, the flow of the form is very logical, with everything happening in the order that you would expect.

Form 1040EZ

If you meet a handful of requirements, you'll be allowed to file Form 1040EZ instead of a regular Form 1040. To be eligible to file Form 1040EZ you must:

- Be either single or married filing jointly;
- Be under age 65 at the end of the tax year;
- Have less than $100,000 of taxable income for the year;
- Not claim any above the line deductions;
- Not claim any credits aside from the earned income credit; and

- Have earned only the following types of income: wages, salaries, tips, unemployment compensation, taxable scholarships, or less than $1,500 of interest.

Schedules for Form 1040

In the field of taxation, a "schedule" is an attachment to a "form." Most schedules that you'll hear about are attachments to your Form 1040. The most frequently used schedules include:

Schedule A: If you plan to itemize, this schedule is where you will list and sum all of your itemized deductions.

Schedule B: This schedule is used to report interest and dividend income. Generally, you won't be required to fill it out unless you've received more than $1,500 of interest or dividends.

Schedule C: If you run a business as a sole proprietor, you will use this schedule to calculate and report your business's profit or loss.

Schedule D: Used to report capital gains and losses.

Schedule E: Used to report income (or loss) from rental real estate, royalties, partnerships, S-corporations, estates, or trusts.

How to Know Which Form(s) and Schedules to Use

You won't have any trouble determining which forms or schedules you have to fill out. Simply proceed line-by-line through your Form 1040, and when you need to fill out an additional form or schedule, it will usually be stated right on your 1040.

For example, if you have income from a business, you'll see that right on Form 1040, line 12 ("business income or loss") you are asked to attach Schedule C or C-EZ.

Chapter 10 Simple Summary

- Most likely, Form 1040 is the primary form you'll be filling out every year. If you meet certain requirements, however, you can file the shorter Form 1040EZ.

- Don't worry about memorizing the purpose of each individual form or schedule. When you need to fill out an additional form or schedule, it will generally say so right on your Form 1040 or in the accompanying instructions.

CHAPTER ELEVEN

State Income Taxes

It's likely that, in addition to federal income tax, you're responsible for paying income tax to your state as well. While income tax rates vary from state to state, the general premise is the same (with, of course, the exception of the handful of states that have no income tax).

How it Works in Most States

Most state income tax returns are short and easy to prepare. Rather than making you go through another calculation to determine your taxable income from scratch, they simply allow you to enter your taxable income from your federal Form 1040.

Your taxable income from your federal return is then usually subjected to a few adjustments—if, for example, your state doesn't allow deductions for certain expenses that are deductible for federal purposes. After making these adjustments, you can generally calculate your state income tax for the year by looking up your taxable income in a table that's provided in the form's instructions.

The most common complicating factor for a state tax return is living and working in multiple states over the course of a year. But it's nothing to worry about. You simply have a little more paperwork to do, as each state will require you to fill out an extra form to calculate how much of your income was earned while working in that state as opposed to other states.

Where to Look for Information

One thing that can make state taxation somewhat more challenging is the fact that information about the topic is generally less accessible. Many states' Department of Revenue websites leave much to be desired. They're often hard to navigate, with nearly useless built-in search functions. As a result, it frequently takes a little more work than you'd expect to find the answers to questions.

One useful tip for finding information on hard-to-navigate websites is to use Google to search that specific site for a given term. For example, dor.mo.gov is the website for Missouri's Department of Revenue. If you wanted to search that site for information about tax filing deadlines, you could enter the following search into Google:

site:dor.mo.gov tax filing deadlines

Or, if you wanted to search the website of the Illinois Department of Revenue (tax.illinois.gov) for information about tax breaks for paying education expenses, you could run the following Google search:

site:tax.illinois.gov education expenses

Deduction for State Income Taxes

As mentioned in Chapter 7, you're allowed an itemized deduction (on your federal return) for state and local income taxes paid over the course of the year. For example, for 2018 the deduction would include:

- State and local income taxes withheld from your salary over the course of the year,

- State and local income taxes paid during 2018 for a prior year (if, for example, you had to include a check with your 2017 state income tax return), and
- State and local estimated tax payments that you made during 2018.

The deduction for state and local taxes is limited to a total of $10,000 per year. Also, the deduction does not include penalties or interest paid along with those taxes.

EXAMPLE: Melissa files her 2017 state tax return on June 10th of 2018, making it approximately two months late. She has to send a check for $320, $100 of which was for interest and penalties for late filing.

For 2018, Melissa will be able to take an itemized deduction for the $220 in tax that she paid with her 2017 return (in addition to any state and local income taxes that are withheld from her paychecks over the course of 2018). But she will not be able to deduct the $100 she paid for interest and penalties.

Chapter 11 Simple Summary

- Most states charge income taxes based upon a slightly-adjusted version of your taxable income from your federal return. As such, preparing your state tax return will usually be easy after having prepared your federal return.

- Each year, you're allowed an itemized deduction on your federal return for any state and local income taxes that you pay over the course of the year. The deduction for state and local taxes is limited to $10,000 per year.

CHAPTER TWELVE

The Alternative Minimum Tax (AMT)

The idea of the alternative minimum tax is to act as a sort of "catch-all" to prevent high-income taxpayers from being able to take advantage of so many deductions and credits that, despite their high income, they pay very little income tax.

The general premise is simple: Start with your gross income, subtract a large exemption (for 2018, $70,300 for single taxpayers and $109,400 for married taxpayers filing jointly) and subject the remaining income to a 26% tax (28% for amounts over a certain threshold: $191,500 for 2018). This "alternative tax" is then compared to your income tax as calculated by the normal method. Whichever tax is greater is what you are required to pay.[1]

Why Calculating AMT is So Difficult

Given that the basic idea behind the AMT is so simple (income, minus a big exemption, times 26% tax), you'd think that it wouldn't be too hard to calculate. Unfortunately, the actual calculation of the AMT is not so simple.

To calculate the AMT (using Form 6251), you must work backwards. You *start* with your adjusted gross income from your Form 1040. From there you make several adjustments for transactions that are treated differently for regular income tax purposes and AMT purposes, and you add back a few "preference items" (e.g., deductions that were allowed on your regular return that aren't allowed for AMT purposes). The resulting answer is your "alternative minimum taxable income."

From here, you subtract the AMT exemption, and multiply the answer by 26% (28% for

---

[1] If your alternative minimum taxable income exceeds a certain threshold (in 2018, $500,000 for single taxpayers and $1,000,000 for married taxpayers filing jointly), your AMT exemption amount is reduced by 25% of this excess.

amounts over \$191,500). The resulting figure (your "tentative minimum tax") is compared to your regular income tax, and you are required to pay the greater of the two.

Chapter 12 Simple Summary

- If you're subject to the AMT, either hire a professional, or be ready to spend plenty of time preparing your tax return.

- Calculating your alternative minimum taxable income involves working backwards from your adjusted gross income, making several adjustments, adding back a few "preference" items, and subtracting a large exemption. Your AMT is then determined based upon the result of these calculations.

CONCLUSION

Do It Yourself or
Find a Tax Professional?

An important question you'll have to answer each year is whether you plan to do your tax preparation yourself or find a professional to take care of it for you. As you can imagine, several factors should be considered.

In my opinion, however, one factor really trumps the rest: Do you even *want* to do it on your own? If preparing your own tax return sounds like a terrible experience to you, in all honesty, you're probably right. Also, if you're just trying to rush through it, you're more likely to make a mistake or miss a deduction that you could have taken.

If, on the other hand, you think you're the type who might find this sort of thing enjoyable, go ahead and give it a try. It's bound to be an educational experience, as it's practically impossible to prepare your own tax return without learning something in the process. Using software such as TurboTax is obviously very popular (for good reason), though you will probably learn more by actually working through the forms on your own.

Furthermore, if you attempt to do it on your own, and you eventually decide that you're just not cut out for it, that's fine. You shouldn't have any trouble finding a tax professional to finish off an already-started return. Similarly, if you prepare your own return but aren't completely confident in your abilities, it's absolutely reasonable to take it to a professional and pay a fee to get the return checked over to see if you missed anything.

But even if you do prepare your own return, don't write off the idea of finding a competent tax professional. Where a high quality tax professional really shows his/her worth isn't with tax preparation. The biggest advantage gained by having a tax advisor is that he or she will often be able to find something that you could be doing differently in order to save yourself some money. And, frequently, these are things that you probably wouldn't catch just by doing your own tax return.

In summary, if you want to prepare your own return this year—or every year—go right ahead. You'll likely learn a lot, and you'll certainly save yourself some money on accounting fees. It would still be wise, however, to develop a working relationship with a tax advisor whom you can trust with more complicated situations.

APPENDIX

Helpful Online Resources

www.irs.gov
> The IRS's website. Has an abundance of surprisingly understandable information.

www.ObliviousInvestor.com
> The author's blog. Includes a wide variety of investing and tax-related articles.

www.Bogleheads.org/forum
> An online forum (named after the founder of Vanguard) with an active group of users with expertise on a range of personal finance topics.

IRS Publications

Publication 503 – Child and Dependent Care Expenses

Publication 550 – Investment Income and Expenses

Publication 596 – Earned Income Credit

Taxes Made Simple: Income Taxes
Explained in 100 Pages or Less

Publication 526 – Charitable Contributions

Publication 970 – Tax Benefits for Education

Publication 502 – Medical and Dental Expenses

Publication 559 – Survivors, Executors, and
    Administrators

A Note on IRS Publications

Throughout the book, I reference various IRS
publications, as I believe that they're a helpful
source of information for most taxpayers. Please
note, however, that IRS publications do not have
any legal authority. So, for example, if the information in an IRS publication contradicts the
information in the actual Internal Revenue Code,
it is the Code that wins.

About the Author

Mike Piper is the author of several personal fi-
nance books as well as the popular blog Oblivi-
ousInvestor.com. He is a Missouri licensed CPA.
Mike's writing has been featured in many places,
including *The Wall Street Journal*, *Money*, *Forbes*,
MarketWatch, and *Morningstar*.

Also by Mike Piper:

Accounting Made Simple: Accounting Explained in 100 Pages or Less

Can I Retire? How to Manage Your Retirement Savings, Explained in 100 Pages or Less

Cost Accounting Made Simple: Cost Accounting Explained in 100 Pages or Less

Independent Contractor, Sole Proprietor, and LLC Taxes Explained in 100 Pages or Less

Investing Made Simple: Investing in Index Funds Explained in 100 Pages or Less

LLC vs. S-Corp vs. C-Corp Explained in 100 Pages or Less

Microeconomics Made Simple: Basic Microeconomic Principles Explained in 100 Pages or Less

Social Security Made Simple: Social Security Retirement Benefits Explained in 100 Pages or Less

INDEX

Made in the USA
San Bernardino, CA
07 March 2019